Leadership: The 5 Fundamentals for Restaurant Managers

By Brent Boso

Thank you to my loving wife Amanda.

Mom & Dad for raising me well.

Angel & Carlene Rosado for all of their help.

Chris Schenck for paving the way.

Sean Raistrick for leadership coaching and additional editing.

All friends and family for support and patience over the years.

Original cover and backing design by Roland Ali P.

<u>PREFACE</u>

If you feel useless at work, this book will help you get busy. If you feel overloaded, this book will help you achieve better organization and more free time. Build important skills to be a strong leader. Wield confidence and be the go-to person to get things done. Go to work feeling good and then come home feeling great. Even if it may or may not be your long-term career choice, the skills are the fundamentals of any job no matter what you wish to become.

My main purpose is to teach newer and struggling managers to be great leaders in the Quick-Service industry. People who have leadership characteristics are thrown into the scary world of management and are immediately expected to know how run a restaurant perfectly. Their leadership skills are never grown and in result they're not setup to succeed. Simply put: It doesn't work that way. Do you think Michael Jordan just picked up a basketball one day and suddenly was a Hall of Famer? With anything in life, if you want to be remotely good at something compared to other people, it takes a lot of self-discipline, practice, and determination. It's hard to do any of that if you don't have a good understanding of what to do or where to start. This book is a tool to get you rolling with the basics of management, and at the same time go into a level of detail that will help even experienced managers sharpen their skills and push their expectations to a new level.

It's time to look inside yourself and see what you can do. Stop dreaming about becoming a better leader and let's actually do it!

Table of Contents

Chapter 1: (Introductory) Know Your Role

What is a manager?

A manager is the driving force of everybody around them. A manager is the master of all positions. A manager is always willing to coach others and is equally excited to learn new things. A manager takes a dull moment and makes it time for teaching, or gets everybody focused during a busy moment. Most importantly, a manager is a leader. A manager is all of these things and much, much more. But most people don't feel this way about their job. How do you get to this status of an awe-inspiring manager at your Quick-Service location? Take a deep breath and let's start at the basics.

What does "manage" even mean? Since this book will be a hard look at the fundamentals, let's just look at the definition of the word "manage."

Man-age

verb (used with object)
1. to bring about or succeed in accomplishing, sometimes despite difficulty or hardship.

2. to take charge or care of.

3. to dominate or influence (a person) by tact, flattery, or artifice.

Sounds basic enough, right? Most managers I've met, particularly young managers, have a general idea of what managing means, but not its exact definition. In other words: hard to put into a sentence. Try your best to remember what the word "manage" really means. After all, it is the title of your job. This way you won't say that vague term "I'm a manager," without knowing what to say afterwards. It makes your job sound lame and boring, when really it's not. Next time, you should try saying something like: "I'm a manager at my restaurant. I step in when things get hard and take control, but I mostly try to influence people to become better at their job."

If it sounds so basic, why are most Quick-Service restaurants run so poorly? I don't know about you, but I have had way more bad experiences at these restaurant types than good ones. I think most people do. Being inside the business, I see it's a problem that doesn't start from the bottom to the top, but rather from the top to the bottom. It's the management that leads and holds expectations for their co-workers. But when the management team isn't capable, then the whole team and the restaurant suffers.

Poorly run restaurants have managers who are only trained to put out fires, rather than taking a true leadership role and figuring out what started the fire. Then taking that information and making sure those fires never start again.

Actively using the fundamentals of management can be the difference between bad and good, or good and great. The learning process of the fundamentals taught in this book aren't necessarily hard, but it's the act of doing them is where most people fail. The transition of becoming a leader is difficult. When promoted you don't suddenly gain the innate human ability to lead. It takes time, patience, and a lot of effort. Some of the reasons why managers don't perform well in their role could be, but are not limited to: a lack of motivation, organization, goals, accountability, a will to teach others, teamwork, and/or communication. Do you have some of these issues? We'll tackle all of these and get you through the basics of management. Even if you have a few years of management under your belt, it never hurts to get motivated and fine-tune your leadership skills.

Simply better understanding your role is a big accomplishment some managers don't achieve. You're already one step closer to greatness. It's the first step to you must take in order to really *get* any other fundamentals. This is what we're going to focus on. It may sound rudimentary, but it is extremely important to understand why you are manager before you actually do anything. Think about it: If you were going to build the Empire State Building, you wouldn't start at the top. You'd start at the bottom. You have to understand *what* it is your building before you actually build it. If you don't have the fundamentals down, your building will tumble to the ground.

Fitting In – Where is Your Place: A manager can be challenged when it comes to feeling comfortable in a hierarchy. You are a boss to several people and at the same time you have bosses to listen to. All the while you have a handful of other managers on the same playing field as you. It takes a lot of teamwork and communication to run a restaurant like that. Let's briefly talk about how your manager role affects some of the positions of a standard hierarchy filled with regular employees, managers, and bosses.

Your Role with Standard Employees: The manager role with regular employees is all about balance. There's a fine line between being a friendly boss and a strict boss. Being too friendly can often times hide the fact that you're their boss, and being too strict is a good way to scare them out of the door. Going heavy on either side is going to result in lost respect for who you are at your job – that's not good. With regular employees, you absolutely have to achieve that balance. You can't just chat it up and have a fun time during every slow moment. Sometimes – more often than not -- you have to hunker down and take that valuable time and teach them something or get things stocked. At the same time, getting to know employees past an interview and a basic introduction can be used as a strength as well. Find that balance and you'll have a great work relationship with your coworkers. For more about approaching team members, look into Chapter 4: Educating Others.

Your Role with Other Managers: The role you play with other managers is the most complicated and delicate work relationship you will have. Not only do you need to treat them as equals, but you will also listen to and be listened to. The icing on this delicious relationship cake is holding them accountable, and them to you as well. Whether that means you're confronting the manager themselves or going to your general manager about an issue, it can be most drama-inducing part of your job.

My recommendation to all management is to do whatever you can to help each other out if asked to – even if it's not technically your job. At the same time, you shouldn't go around and do another person's job for them. Maybe they're slacking, but it's still their job – not yours. If you quietly pick up the slack for everyone without being asked, you're getting your foot in the door for a bunch of drama. What if you planned to get a small project done on Thursday, and another manager thought you were slacking and did it for you? You probably wouldn't feel too happy about it, even though it's less work for you to do. Don't intentionally go out of your way to make someone else look bad. You wouldn't appreciate that at all, would you?

Another tip for tending to relationships with other managers is to check your attitude and emotions at the door. Think strictly business and what's best for the store. This doesn't mean you have to be a robot and can't talk shop with anyone. But when the team is discussing business matters, don't instantly get emotionally involved (defensive) with every situation. Think what's best for the store, fight for that, but don't be afraid to lose.

This is where a lot of people fail: being prepared to lose and not have things go your way. Yes, you think might have thought of the best idea ever that's going to turn the restaurant into the highest quality and fastest running establishment it could be. Guess what? It will absolutely not work if you can't get the team to support you. Additionally, you're not the only one who works here. Losing, sometimes, can be okay.

In my experience, attitude is offensive and emotions are usually defensive. A typical manager **attitude** says things like, "Wow, I can do that job better than that person." And a common **emotional** manager says, "Why did you teach Harry how to order produce? I wanted to do that." Now usually the manager with an attitude has never even done that job before, or when they did they weren't perfect either. And the defensive manager never communicated to the other managers what their plans were, and it shouldn't be anyone's fault for wanting to teach an employee a new skill.

If you invest your feelings into what other people do, then you will get hurt and hurt others. Instead, stay calm and professional. Don't whine about something going wrong behind another person's back – go to that person and nicely ask them about the situation. The second you're saying things like "I can't stand when X person does Y thing. It really ticks me off," to another person or manager, then you're just a part of the drama problem. Don't just complain behind the person's back. Help actually solve the issue by confronting them nicely.

Unless the reason is blatant, try not to confront other managers about little things just to make it a big deal. If built up enough, drama can be the true killer of even the best teams. Remember that you guys are a team at all times. Have sympathy for each other during hard times or failures, and do your best to give feedback on ideas and back each other up. We all make mistakes. You're not perfect either. We all have days where we aren't going to give it our best. We're all human. Pick and choose your battles – don't be fighting all of the time. Just a little rip in a piece of paper can tear the whole thing apart. Always remember that.

Your Role with Your Boss/Bosses: Thankfully, the relationships between you and your bosses are quite short and simple: Do what you're told to do on time; never complain; and ask questions if you're uncertain about anything. It takes time, but your goal is to build trust with your bosses and be the go-to guy or gal about anything. If you were the GM or owner, you should feel comfortable going to a manager and asking them to do something. For instance, if a manager is asked to come up with a new cleaning plan and get it rolling ASAP, it shouldn't be a month-long project. They probably want it to be completed and shown to them in a few days. That may mean you have to stay late or come in early to get it done, but that's what it takes to stand out. It only takes one or two times for you to let your boss down, and then you're not looking trustworthy as a manager. Mostly likely they'll skip your name when it comes to the next task that needs delegation.

Also, take advantage of "extra mile" moments. Use those moments when you see a situation you can benefit by helping out. For instance, if you overhear talk about being short-staffed for a special event, go to them and offer to stay. Obviously, this is also applicable to your co-managers if you are having relationship issues with them. You don't have to be the person to step up every single time, but when it gives you a big relationship benefit then you should take advantage of that opportunity.

Simply enough: just do what you're told, be timely, and don't complain to your bosses and you'll do just fine.

Your Driving Role to the Restaurant – Vision & Initiative

Store Vision: What is your store vision? Talk with your bosses and ask them, "What is our store vision?" Each restaurant will have different goals. Perhaps the current store vision is to have the #1 customer service in your state. So then the next question is, "What is our plan to achieve that?" or "What is our store philosophy or business model that will guide us to reach our goal?" Lastly, be sure that you ask them "How do we tell if we're succeeding or failing? What tools do we use to measure our goal progress?"

The idea is to discover the bigger picture, and think big picture during 100% of your work day. If your store's goals revolve around labor, it will help you make decisions to send people home during slow moments. If it's rather about growing sales, then training and reinforcing the team will be your goal during those moments.

Figure out your overall goal. When you know your boss's goal, then you find your goals as well. Use your restaurant's goals to help you motivate and prioritize your workload. Remember that everything you do leads to that big picture goal. This will help prevent you from feeling detached from the store and make you feel part of the leadership team.

Your Role as a Leader: What am I doing every single day to help push the restaurant in a better direction than it is now? Does this follow your restaurant's "vision?"

The answer shouldn't be some elaborate story about only one big project that's going to change the face of your whole restaurant. It should be the little things, all day and every day. Service, speed, and cleanliness will cover most aspects of what a guest experiences. This is what we'll focus on in this little sub-chapter here; not necessarily the broad idea of managing, but the day-to-day drive and focus of it.

You are the driving force of everyone around you every single day. It's very important to realize that and accept the responsibility. If you're goofing off and just doing the bare minimum to get through the day, then that's the amount of pay, respect, and overall personal growth you'll receive. Although we'll discuss pay and self-motivation in Chapter 2: Self-Goals, it's crucial to at least understand this: there are only a few people capable of doing your job. Think about it, is a basic team member with basic training going to realize he or she can use a slow moment to check-up on all of the guests in the dining room? Of course not. They also won't see that the Drive-Thru is moving slow and could use a hand. They won't grab a towel and start an overdue cleaning project. They're most likely going to stand around and chat with other employees.

You squash that from happening. You keep everyone focused. Every hour of every day you work. That is your job. That is the number one way of how you come from the bottom and work your way to the top of management.

This is the overall tone this book will carry. There's a good reason to that! My goal is to have you absorb that feeling of focus and drive, and then carry it into work with you. If you're really gung-ho about pushing the restaurant, then a lot of those bad habits you may have should disappear – or at the very least you will catch yourself in the moment.

"What are these bad habits you're talking about?"

The bad habit of being unfocused and not pushing some aspect of the store.

Chatting with employees about various topics while getting nothing else done; playing on your phone; refilling your drink for the 8th time in the last hour; disappearing from your position for a little too long; etc.

Instead here are six of the several things you could be doing JUST in your dining room:

SERVICE	CLEANLINESS
Clearing Guest's Trays	Cleaning Tables
Providing Refills	Spot Checking Windows for Fingerprints
Offer Mints or Other Novelties	Sweeping Floors
Open the Door for the Next Guest/Immediately Greet Them	Making Sure All Signs & Menu Boards Are Clean
Setting Tables for Guests (Straws/Napkins/Etc)	Scrubbing Down Any Obscene Stains On Walls/Chairs/Tables
Setting Up Highchairs/Other Needs for Parents with Children	Checking Bathroom Toiletries & Quality

Handing Tasks Off: With all of this focus-talk, there is one important word to remember: Delegation. You absolutely need to be delegating nearly all of the work that needs to be done. It's a hard mental-barrier to get through if you're used to doing everything yourself. That's especially true if you have an "I can do it quicker or better than anyone else" mentality. Not saying that's false. I know I can do almost all of the tasks in the store quicker, better, neater than nearly anyone else in the store. I'm sure you can too. To those people I say, "Get over yourself." Yeah, that's right. Get over yourself. I used to think the same way, and I'm glad I got out of it. When you're the person who does absolutely everything, it just hurts the team when you're not there. Your team's progress slows to a crawl.

Thanks to delegating almost everything that needs to get stocked, cleaned, or just taken care of, my team grew and got better at doing these tasks. Over time, a whole team of people who can get the store stocked and cleaned will do it several times faster than just one or two managers. Of course at first you have to suffer and deal with someone taking two or three times longer than they should, but they'll eventually get faster about it as long as you push them. It helps to give time limits for everything. For instance, if I hand off a dressing container to be stocked within 5 minutes, I make sure that I let that person know the expectation. It doesn't take much, just glance at the clock and quickly let them know "I want you back up here by 2:57, okay?" Otherwise you can expect them to take their time and not feel rushed.

Your role should not be the manager zipping around the restaurant trying to do everything yourself. Your role should be the conductor who leads others in the right direction all of the time. Of course, each restaurant is different from each other. Think about how you run things now, and apply what you've read to your particular situation. What could you do differently? Restaurants with smaller teams might demand more from the manager and they might need to be more involved in stocking, cleaning, etc. Bigger teams should allow the manager to able to run the store without leaving a position, if they're tied to a position at all.

In the end, find thirty minutes to talk with your bosses and figure out how they envision you running the restaurant. Getting on the same page can be the start of a great future. Do they want a hybrid of delegation and you also pitching in? Would they rather have you possess a more "lead from the front" type mentality in which you delegate nearly everything?

Obvious as it sounds, it certainly helps knowing what and how you're supposed to be doing. It's the first fundamental of management, and often the most looked over. It's sometimes never clearly explained how to be a leader. In the industry we work in, it's common to become fast and friendly at a job and be promoted. However, leadership quality (and it's teaching of) can easily be forgotten. When the manager is depended to control the restaurant and its people, sometimes that lack of understanding your role can show. When it shows, it shows to your bosses, your coworkers and your guests.

Find your purpose at your restaurant and be great at it. Manage problems and lead the people around you. Know your role!

Chapter 1 "Know Your Role" Conclusion:

- Truly **define** your job. Be able to **form a clear sentence** about what **your role** is. **Write** it down or **say** it out loud.
- **Think** about your restaurant's hierarchy. How should **you fit in** professionally? Are there others **below** you, on the **same** level, or **higher** than you? Be sure your relationship with **each** "category" of coworkers is **true to your role**.
- Get simple and **think** about what you do every day to help **drive the focus** of the restaurant. Think about how you **affect** what the guest **sees**: service, speed, and cleanliness. Remember that **every moment you have** should be spent pushing **at least one** of these aspects of the store.

- If your restaurant's staff size allows it, **delegate** as many tasks as possible to **other employees**. **Conduct** and **lead** the staff; don't do everything yourself.
- When delegating, be sure to make your **expectations** clear. Give **time limits**, and make sure the employee knows **exactly** how you want the task done.
- **Talk** with your boss and see if how you're working **matches up** with **their vision of your role.** Make changes to your **everyday actions** as needed.

Chapter 2: Self Goals

At the time of this writing I've been in the quick-service industry for nearly a decade. I remember my first year as a manager being pretty rough. It's funny looking back at it. I was very young and never wanted to learn anything new. I thought I was great at my job just because I was a manager. In retrospect, it's a little embarrassing. I never motivated anyone around me. I never taught people as much as I should have. I sometimes moved people around and gave direction, but not without much care or passion behind it. I certainly was the last person you wanted to come to about a mistake or a problem, even if it was my own fault.

I just wanted to go home. My real dream was – and still is to this very day – to become a video game critic. Yeah, it is a real job title. The video game industry is flourishing day-by-day, and I've always been in love with it. I've had fun writing, and I love video games and the people inside the industry. Why not try to make a living from it? At the time I wrote for a small website and was extremely devoted to it. I wanted it to blow up into something popular. I was never paid and were the games weren't freely supplied to me. It took an amazing amount of my time, money, I wasn't really gaining anything from it other than the experience.

I quit my management job at my local Quick-Service restaurant. A little while later, I finally left the web site I wrote for. During my leave my boss acquired a new, more upscale and promising location. It'd be literally 6 to 7 times busier and being a manager there would be a much bigger deal. You could say we made it to the big leagues. When I got my job back a little bit after the store's grand opening, I really don't think I cut it. I still had all of my old habits. I was at a point in my life where paychecks were a nice thing to have, but not a necessity. I was a nice guy and was good at giving orders. I was growing, but definitely had a long way to go.

There was a problem. I'm still the same person now, so why was I a bad manager back then? There was definitely a missing link in the chain somewhere.

I had no goals.

I had nothing driving me to become better. I liked my job, but I didn't *love* it. The store was being run by successful managers who were pushing everything and everyone around me. They made good money, and seemed a lot more satisfied than I was; even with more responsibilities on their shoulders. They didn't need me to step up. I'm sure they wanted me to, but it felt hard to get my foot in that door. I felt like there was a club called "Super Awesome People Who Are Amazing at Their Jobs," and it wasn't looking for any more members.

Turns out clubs like that will hardly ever look for new members. The reality is that you have to bust your ass and work hard to get into that club. Nowadays I run that club and I train the people within it.

Upon realizing that I needed to do something, I started paying closer attention to how they worked. I'd call it something along the lines of OCD, but every little detail mattered to me. It wasn't just watching those managers work a position – no – that wasn't the only thing I was focused on. I was more into the words and phrasing of how they taught, delegated tasks, and moved people around the store. It sounds lame, but I began to copy them and added a little bit of my own personality and style to everything I did. It took a while, but it was my "Manager's First Steps," so to speak.

Not too long after those days my General Manager put me through a leadership training program. He, himself, taught me the fundamentals and helped me with the basics of managing. The training module itself made me realize there was so much more to my job that I was missing. Not physical things that I didn't know how to do, but more of a mental state and _what_ a manager really was supposed to be. A-ha, an epiphany! I didn't know what to do beforehand. All they gave me was a shirt and a tie and taught me how to count money. During the training I was overwhelmed by how much more there was to this job. I wasn't just some manager at a fast food restaurant making $9.00 an hour. I was becoming a manager at a living and breathing multi-million dollar restaurant that helps thousands of guests per day – and I still wanted to be more than that.

I wanted to get better. It was a vague goal, but it was a goal nonetheless.

Here came the intensity that almost always follows an epiphany: I became so passionate about everything I did. I wanted to take on everything. Order accuracy issues we were having; the overall customer experience; training plans; mastering positions; planning/organizing the day, etc. You could say that I was the ant who just discovered it could carry 10 times its weight and then tried carrying a whole house.

Regardless of where my head was, it was now at least in a direction moving forward. Having some sort of goal in my head drove me. Every day I drove to work I thought to myself "How can I be even better today?" Eventually that goal was shifted to another one – my first real goal. I went to my GM and said, "In 6 months, I want to be making $1.50 more. What can I be doing right now to make that happen?" It was gutsy because it was a huge leap in wage. Thankfully, my bosses do their best to believe in "equal work means equal pay." As long as it's not unreasonable, that's their bottom line and it's a damn good one.

We chatted several times over the course of a few months. We talked about different day parts and how to handle them. What our strengths and weaknesses were as a team. What my personal strengths and weaknesses were. There were things said that made me proud, angry, upset, happy – you name it. It was a lot to take in at once, but it helped shift me closer to my goal. It was a real eye-opening experience. I'm glad I was patient and understanding at the time and soaked it all in, because it really molded me into the person – not just the leader – I am today.

I took on new responsibilities and was really psyched about being more involved in the business. We finally found a role for me – even if it felt like a small one. I managed our customer survey results and tried to correct weaknesses of the store. I did this for only about three months before moving onto bigger things. Every couple weeks I'd try to see how I was doing by checking in with my GM. We would tweak a few things here and there. We would bounce new ideas off of each other. I'd do my best to follow through with what we talked about.

Now that I'm on the other side of leadership, I'll tell you that going to your boss on your own time truly shows that you have potential and passion. Don't wait for them to come to you – that's what everybody else does.

To wrap up my personal story, I met my wage goal 2 months early. I immediately set another identical goal, and met that one early too. Nowadays, I have so many different goals that it's mind-boggling. Big goals like wage increases and projects that will take weeks or months to complete. Small goals like cleaning projects, or teaching a specific person a specific task. Regardless of the size of the goal, every time I drive to my store, I think hard about how I'll achieve them. Most importantly, every time I do complete a goal I get a little burst of energy, motivation, and a sense of accomplishment. It's the fuel that keeps the fire going.

Take a moment and think about yourself. How do you fit in with this scenario? Do you have abstract goals? Concrete goals? Easy goals? Difficult goals? Do you have any goals at all? Maybe outside of work you have a goal to read a book every month. Or maybe you're great at finances and have weekly budget goals that keep you motivated?

What about inside of work? We're going to nail this down and find you a motivational goal. The idea is to increase your own performance while also making work a little more exciting.

Goal Crafting

A manager without goals is like an airplane with no wings. What's the point?

What goal would motivate yourself at work? It's a question you'll have to answer on your own. The "wage increase" goal is very motivating for most people. Since the first time I had that goal, I've continuously reset it higher and higher each time I achieved it. I think this is a great first goal and can be a re-energizing. Everyone wants to feel like their worth a good

18

amount of money and a lot of people would love to have more of it.

Perhaps money isn't the primary desire at this time in your life. Maybe you feel bored at work and want to do more? What about a goal to take over some responsibility? It could be that you have a hunger to do a little more around the restaurant. Being involved in a role that comes with bigger tasks can help you feel excited to work. It helps you feel important to the team and gives you something else to do. But what is that role?

Does talking to potential employees, interviewing, and orientation get you excited about your job? Look at it as being the sole person responsible for finding the best people for the restaurant. If that's the case, you should talk to your GM and get on a plan to becoming a "Hiring Manager" of some sort. That way if the restaurant needs to hire anyone, you're the go-to manager.

Or maybe you've always been interested in some back-house work such as scheduling or ordering inventory? Being responsible with tasks that keep the store running without issues can make you feel very vital to the store's success. Again, you should talk to your GM and try to see how you can get on that path.

Don't be afraid of approaching someone who's in charge with the idea of taking a responsibility. Either two things will happen:

1.) The first is that they will try to get you on a plan almost right away, because I believe most GMs are overloaded with work and will try to delegate it to other people if the opportunity arises. They might stress over the initial fact that you will need to be trained, and that will cause more work, but in the long-term it'll be beneficial. Be ready though, because you might get a responsibility you aren't very excited about. The goal is to succeed with that task to get to the real ones you would like to do.

Or...

2.) They say you're not ready yet. Not what you wanted to hear, but ultimately it is part of the overall plan. Maybe you have other things to work on first. Micro-managing people and the store itself; overall leadership skill; showing up to work on time; relationships with other managers; attitude around work; etc. They will give you reasons, and you NEED to remember them! This is the learning opportunity that you should be writing down and taking seriously. Ask a lot of questions. Each point they make, ask "How can I get better with that?" This alone will show them you mean business and that you actually want to improve yourself.

Try your best to not get upset at the second response - this is fine.

Before you take on responsibilities, you need to take care of minor self-issues first. Otherwise, you might severely hurt your chances later on. The last thing your boss would like is for you to take over scheduling, and then you don't get the job done. If that were to happen, you could consider yourself pretty much blacklisted from any responsibilities for a long time since you're considered untrustworthy. At that point, good luck trying to make more money and meeting your goals. Shooting yourself in the foot is not a good start to a marathon.

So don't take it personal if that is the response you get. Make it clear to your boss that you want to be on the path to that destination. You'll work on what was discussed, and then come back to find more things to work on. Maybe you'll get that responsibility in a few months if you work hard at it. Correcting any issues you seem to have at work is all a part of walking that path. Sometimes the process can take a little while – be patient, even if the path feels like the scenic route.

Wage increase and gaining responsibility are two basic goals you have in front of you. You may find other goals depending on your job and some goals may even find you. However, there is much more to goal crafting than just picking something and going for it. Whatever your goal is, don't make it abstract and inexpressible. You need to be able to pin it down and form a clear sentence that makes sense. In order to form that sentence, we're going to need to talk about one other aspect of goal crafting: Obtainability.

You want your main goal to be not too far out of your reach, but at the same time to make you feel accomplished when you finish it. Too small of a goal and it won't be rewarding enough. Too big of a goal and you might never achieve it. The first step about obtainability is to take a hard, true, and objective look at yourself and ask "What am I capable of? What goal is right for me?" Your boss will be doing the same thing. To help you see yourself through the eyes of your boss, you probably fit into one of these three categories:

1. **(High Capability) - You feel like an incredible asset to the store.** You go above and beyond just counting registers and opening or closing the restaurant. Driving the team and teaching coworkers comes natural and you enjoy it. You may or

may not have a good amount of responsibility, but you get it all done in a timely manner. You are a go-to employee and have good relationships with everyone else in the store. You most likely already do your best to help your boss and management team as much as possible.

2. (Medium Capability) - You come to work, but sometimes it's a drag. You might intend to give your best work, but your actual work doesn't fully represent that. You're not the worst employee in the world or anything, and at least you can consistently do the basics. Open, closing, and counting some registers. You make moves when you see them, but that's all you really do. You probably feel best when you are managing by yourself, being able to make decisions without other managers questioning your moves. At the same time, you don't necessarily mind taking a backseat and letting others run the store around you. Overall, you are hit and miss.

3. (Low Capability) - Something doesn't feel right. Your shifts feel incredibly long and boring. You rarely get chances to prove yourself, and sometimes when you do it doesn't happen the way you expected it to. You might be a manager, but when you walk in to your store it's already running well and you feel like you're not a contributing factor. Not "fitting in" is probably a good way to explain this. If you're lucky, other managers are trying to work with you. But they might feel like you're not committing 100%. In the back of your mind you want to meet some level of success, but you're not sure how to get there.

Do you fall into one of these categories? Maybe you're squeezed in between a category or have a little bit of each going on. I can't pin down who you are without ever meeting you.

That's why it's your job to evaluate yourself realistically. It's very important. Why?

Your boss will do the same thing. Isn't it better to take a good look at yourself before you sit down with your boss and ask for more pay? Analogy time: If you went to your English teacher for an important recommendation letter, you'd need to be sure all the work you've done so far is sound. If your work wasn't too great, you'd want to wait a little longer and write a few high-quality essays to show off before making your way to the teacher.

Where you evaluate yourself at is important to your overall goal obtainability. Think of it as a ladder: If you're on the 2nd step and your goal is to get to the 7th step, then first you have 5 more steps to go. Don't think you can just easily skip all of those steps, because you'll just wind up falling on your ass!

While I touched on this earlier, I'd like to repeat this very quickly: The problem I've seen often and have committed myself is that we aim too high or low. Too high, and the goal will beat you down and discourage you. Too low, and it may not be incentive to get your gears going. That's because we think of a goal and immediately make that first "version" of the goal. We don't take the extra time to really think about whether or not it's achievable or not, or if it's going to be worth doing. Go in with a plan – don't just pick something and go in blind.

Going in Blind: You sit down with your boss wanting to get on the track of a $1.00 raise in six months, but your self-evaluation somewhere between a Low-Medium obtainability.

Going in with a Plan: Lower the dollar amount to something more achievable like $0.50, which is probably more appropriate to your obtainability. Alternatively, you could keep the $1.00 goal but aim for six months instead. Meanwhile, you work on the skills needed to be between a Medium-High obtainability. This means you realize you have a lot of work to do.

So be careful about your goal crafting. Having clear-cut goals is a great way to get on track for self-improvement. Otherwise, what are you aiming for at the end of the day? And if you're not aiming for something, then why aren't you?

Goal Hunting, Effort, and Your Future

Probably the biggest excuse I've heard for not trying hard enough is that "Well this isn't my real job, I want to become a lawyer." Of course, "lawyer" can be many other occupations: Police officer, teacher, nurse, chef, software designer, etc. What do you want to be? Maybe you even want to become your very own GM or restaurant owner someday. My tough-love question is always this: How do you expect to become any of those things if you can't master the simplicities of a management job?

This much I've learned: Effort is a key word to succeeding in life. I'm not a millionaire, a doctor or anything like that. However, I do work around people who put in more effort and less effort than others. I've worked with them for several years and I can see why they're in the position they're at – high or low. The hardest working ones who put the most effort into their work lead and manage, while the ones who don't will follow the leaders. It's obvious that the more time and effort you put into any type of work, the better results you will receive. Of course, there's a saying: "It's easier said than done." If putting in hard work every day was easy, then everyone would do it and be millionaires with rollercoasters in their backyard. I think Richie-Rich had one.

What you truly have to realize is simply having honest goals will put you ahead of most people, as long as you are serious about them. Your expectations of yourself should be as high as you want them to be, and those alone will carry you to great things. Mine are somewhere around "extremely great manager material." I want to feel like if I left my job, it would be a pretty big impact to my leadership team. It gives me that extra kick in the butt when I'm not feeling 100%. I remember that my expectations of myself are high, so I better get that thing done and not put it off for another day.

As I said before, my ultimate goal is to become a video game critic. My best chance to break into some level of video game journalism is to start my own web site as a portfolio of work. Three or four years ago, I could never imagine investing and starting my own web site. Now it's different. Now I can safely say I've learned so many business management and leadership skills over the last few years that I feel prepared for it. Most importantly, I learned what real effort is. I learned a lot from my job that has nothing to do with writing, video games, or any journalistic values. I know how to succeed if I put my mind to it, because I already do it every single day.

I've seen it proven and really do believe that hard work in any job field, no matter how polar-opposite it is from what you want to do, can actually lead you to success. It's because it may not be the job that matters, but rather the practice of pure effort.

Chapter 2 "Self-Goals" Conclusion:

- **Discover** and **write down** a clear-cut vision of your work-related goals. One or two to start off should suffice.
- **Evaluate** yourself. Be very **honest** and **objective** about where you currently fit in at your job. Maybe even try to be too harsh! Do you have a lot of basics to master still or are you on top of your game? Maybe you're somewhere in the middle? **Relook** at your goal and ask yourself if it has **a fair level of obtainability** based upon your **evaluation.**
- **Approach** your boss and **pitch** your goals. **Tell** your boss that you want to get **on the path to this goal**, and **ask** what **you need to do** in order to **achieve** it.
- Put **REAL effort** into completing your goals. Remember that what you do now **helps you achieve** better things in the **future!**

Chapter 3: Organization

It's time to transition in between breakfast and lunch. Even on the best of days it can be a rough transition. The Drive-Thru is starting to slow down and is calling for your attention. At the same time there are a few people about to start their shift and are not sure where to go or what to do. You've realized that somebody ordered a dessert you forgot to have prepared. You run to the front line to get the customer a refund since the dessert would take 10 minutes to prepare and they don't want to wait. But the Drive-Thru still needs another person and continues to travel at the slow speed. Still, you could use the two people who just clocked on but there aren't any available registers at the time. It's all happening at the same time. Your patience is running thin, and you're about to explode with frustration. You're only one person after all! Does an overwhelming situation like this one sound familiar?

Organization is absolutely the key ingredient to running a smooth restaurant. Without organization, you and your restaurant quickly losses it's professionalism and ability to do the simplest tasks. I've seen the differences between an organized and unorganized restaurant, and I'm sure you have too. Have you ever walked into a restaurant, from a customer's perspective, and felt like you were adding part of the stress that the employees were going through? That's the general idea I'm talking about. We must avoid making guests feel like they are a part of a "problem" at all costs, otherwise they may not come back. At my location, we're very organized when compared to other restaurants. We have systems in place and are all on the same page. I love it because it makes my job easier and I can focus on pushing the restaurant forward rather than just trying to maintain it. However, getting to this point didn't happen overnight. It takes hard work, a good plan, time, and execution. That's what we're going to work on.

Think about yourself for a minute. Are you an organized person at work? If so, what makes you organized? If not, why not? Think back to when you're in the middle of a hectic moment. What could be done afterwards to ensure that it won't happen again, or that it could be handled better? That's the beginning of being organized. If it sounds more like problem solving, think about it like problem solving before the problem even happens.

Ahead, I will explain how to implement organizational skills to not only benefit your restaurant, but also yourself. Within that, I'll give a few examples of basic day-to-day systems to help create your own systems at your restaurant. From there, we'll go over how to get coworkers to support your ideas and get the ball rolling.

Remember that we're not aiming for highly complex ideas – those are hard to think of and are easy to fail. We're looking for simple tools that any manager can use to help themselves and others stay organized. These simple systems should be able to apply to your location, but it will ultimately be your responsibility to develop new ones.

"Any fool can make something complicated. It takes a genius to make it simple."
　　　　　　　　　　　- Woody Guthrie

Also, if the word "system" isn't quite clear, just think of it as another way of saying "a specific way of doing things," or a "way of things taking care of themselves."

From the smallest to the biggest task, it needs to be a part of a system. For example, having the task "Turn on Music Radio" as a part of an opening checklist would help prevent the team forgetting to do it. If you absolutely hate the unorganized chaos and stress that you're put through, then you need to get you and your store organized. Sure, being organized by creating systems doesn't solve 100% of problems. Issues still are going to happen, but they'll be far less common. Regardless, it's safe to say that you and your coworkers will feel less stressed throughout your day.

Organization is not just a magical thing that happens all on its own. It's a mix between brainstorming, teamwork and being proactive. Brainstorming is where the ideas come from; teamwork is having co-workers support it; and being proactive is both making the idea come to life and keeping it alive. Remember that nobody will ever make your ideas come true – you have to do that yourself.

The reward of organization is getting the several tasks out of your head and into some sort of system, like a checklist mentioned before. The more things that are out of your head the less stressed out you'll be. In addition, you'll forget a lot less too. Ever think to yourself "Man, we really need to get [blank] under control," and then a few hours pass and you never think of it again? You most likely only remember when the issue occurs again, but our goal is to prevent issues before they even happen. That's the point of this chapter.

Personal Organization – Notepads & Daily Folder System

Let's Start With You: You can't get a whole team under control and change the ways of doing things if *you're* not even organized. There are several ways you can get yourself on track. It doesn't matter how much responsibility you have; if you're unorganized then even the simplest part of your job can get out of control. Now, prepare yourself for the ultimate secret of being organized and successful at work. Over my years of experience, I really wish I would have been handed down the power I needed in the beginning. Are you ready? Read carefully.

Buy a notepad.

No, really. They're 99 cents in most office supply stores, and they fit right in your pocket. It's the most important physical tool you will have on you in terms of management and leadership. Sounds stupid? Well, all of the obvious things in life are obvious for a reason. But it is the key to never forgetting anything ever again. Keep it on you every day.

Get a freaking notepad. I mean it!

A lot of people will roll their eyes and not take the idea seriously. You need to take it seriously. Notepads are not the turnaround in your life and won't fix every problem and make you the best manager. However, they are the basic tool to getting organized. Tackling a handful of problems every single day is a lot on your mind. As mentioned before, getting that off of your mind and onto paper is the first step to being organized. It's pretty hard to forget things that you wrote down.

What kind of problems should you write down?

Everything and anything you feel like you could make better. Don't overlook the little things. If there have been people taking breaks for too long and you think to yourself "I should post a sign about the break rules," then write something similar down like "Sign: Break Rules on Door" which is a lot better than "Breaks."

Words into Action: Ideas are great, but they're just cool words or thoughts that are scribbled on paper. The exciting part is when you actually turn an idea into reality. Come in early, stay late, or talk to your scheduler to assign you the needed time during your shift. If you ever have a slow moment at the store, use that time effectively and knock out a task or two. It's easy to get things done! However, it's sadly even easier to procrastinate. The mental check of "I need to get some extra work done" is something that doesn't necessarily pop into everyone's head often enough. It's also not easy to want to come in early or late to get work done. But at the same time it's only a few extra hours per week, depending on the size and quantity of the tasks. Think back to possible goals you may have; will this help you achieve them? If the answer is yes then it should feel worth the small amount of time in the grand scheme of things.

In the end, notepads are great! They can be the manager's first tool they truly use to achieve goals. Something so simple that can help you go from a stale manager who just counts drawers, to a manager who is fresh and actively fixes issues. While they are great to keep track of tasks in an on-the-go manner, there are other tools you can utilize as well. If you are in a role that has a handful of office work to do, then you can use a Daily Folder System to help get yourself organized.

Locking It Away for Another Day: A Daily Folder System, or DFS if you're low on time, can help you get on a schedule of doing things at work without the hassle of a calendar. It's a simple way to categorize, prioritize, and organize office work. Also, like the notepad, it'll get things off of your mind and help you feel less overwhelmed. So how does a DFS work?

A DFS is a group of manila folders that each have tasks and days outlined onto them. To put it simple, each folder has certain days of the week on them.

Folder #1 (Monday/Wednesday).
Folder #2 (Tuesday/Thursday/Saturday).
Folder #3 (Friday/Sunday).

Now, think about all of your job's tasks and determine which is the most important that needs to be checked on the most often. You'll want to assign those frequent tasks to the folder with the most days on it, which is Folder #2 in this example. With your other tasks you think of, you'll want them assigned to other folders.

The best part is that the folder's days and tasks are all interchangeable – you make the folders how you see them helping you best. They don't have to be exactly as listed above. It's your job to figure out your tasks and when to do them. If you have only a few things to do a week, you might want fewer folders. Maybe two would work just fine? Or you could have more tasks to do, and maybe even need more folders! Then bump it up to four or five different folders per week.

Now that we have days on these folders, let's break down what we're going to do with them. Let's pretend we're in the role of a scheduler/Human Resources hybrid. Your job tasks may include scheduling, time punch report tracking, customer complaints, interviews, uniform ordering, and tax paperwork, you could lay out your folders like this:

- **Written on Folder #1 (M/W/F): Availability changes (scheduling), customer complaints, and tax paperwork.**

- **Written on Folder #2 (TUE/THU/SAT): Time punch reports, applications (for interviews), and uniform orders.**

Now, remember all that paperwork that you'd get throughout the day regarding your responsibilities? Well, they can go right into these folders. Did you get a new application you need to call for an interview? Put it in Folder #2. Did somebody write down a new availability? Put it in Folder #1. Like your notepad, you should look in your folder of the day before you leave work. So if you're about to head home on Thursday, take a look in your Folder #2 and see if you have any work to do. Work a night shift on Saturday? Come in 20-30 minutes early so you can get your folders taken care of. Or if you see a slow moment, get some work done and take care of it in the middle of your shift.

The reason why this system works is because you're getting things out of your head. It sucks when you're frantically trying to remember everything you have to do throughout the day. Trying to remember "I have to input in those new availabilities, send out those customer complaint letters, and etc." throughout your typical work day just adds stress. Stress can and will lower work performance. Your day is lot easier when you can just think "Oh, I'll check my folder for today before I leave." The work is still the same but the panic and stress of doing it is a lot less.

Going Digital: Another popular way to stay on top of things is to tie an E-mail Account (Gmail, Yahoo) to your smart phone and use the calendar to keep you organized. Depending on your work environment, you may or may not have use of this idea. If you are part of a management team that is large with many responsibilities, it may be a good idea. Communication is one of the most important fundamentals of management. We'll cover the importance of this in Chapter 5. However, since Gmail can help you with personal organization via a computer or smart phone, we'll cover it briefly here.

Note: You can use your phone's personal calendar. Since I use Gmail all of the time, I'll be using that as my example. Replace it with what you have available!

You should have no problems tying your Gmail to your smart phone if you own one. Through Gmail, you can set up calendar events for certain tasks at your store. For instance, if you absolutely have to clean the break room on Monday and Friday, you can put that in your Gmail calendar as an event. You can tell the event to remind you on your smart phone on those days, so that way you don't forget to clean it! Of course, it doesn't have to be cleaning the break room – it can obviously be any of your responsibilities which could be bigger or smaller. Take a few seconds and think about how you might be able to use a calendar/reminder system to help you stay organized.

If you don't have any responsibilities to put into folders, you might want to try to find some! Relating back to Chapter 1: Goals, finding more responsibilities can help you become a better manager and help you meet your long-term goals. So if you have a wage goal you'd like to meet, but don't have any responsibilities, now would be a good time to talk to your boss and find something to do. When you have more on your plate, implementing the DFS can help you stay organized and make sure you won't fail those goals.

When you feel like you've got yourself under control, you can start thinking about the store with a clearer mindset.

Another way of thinking about organization is to think about planning. How often do you plan at work? Planning on-the-go during your shift should take up almost all of your downtime in between rushes. This could mean you're preparing for the next rush, running breaks, or preparing for people to clock off/on. Of course, while organization and planning are keys to the fundamentals of managing, it's often underappreciated and overlooked. What really happens during downtime is usually a lot of talking, sippin' on drinks, and playing around. Of course, it's *your* job to keep that under control. If everyone is talking, then you need to step up. It's okay to have fun at work such as holding a conversation while stocking or cleaning, but simply talking is a bad habit. We will touch base again on this in Chapter 4: Self Accountability.

Planning Can be Simple or Advanced: It can simply be having an area stocked to be ready for the next rush, or it can be a big setup sheet with several plans and actions for the entire day. Each way of planning is equally important. I've seen some restaurants fail to be prepared and handle their busy hours as if they were in a legitimate war – glasses crashing on the ground like grenades and emotions going haywire like a squad in a firefight; it's not only embarrassing for them, but also for the guest. Sometimes we forget where we're at and easily lose our professionalism, which is a whole other topic on its own. Getting properly prepared for the masses of hungry people about to stampede your restaurant is all it takes to keep things under control. Let's focus on a few ways you can get the store organized and ready to run smoothly.

When reading, please keep in mind that restaurants don't always have a common denominator in terms of how they run things. I will try to keep the ideas general. Organization skills that are listed below are structured towards busier restaurants. It's up to you to take the basic ideas and twist them in different ways so they can be used at your store.

Store Organization & Planning – Setup Sheets & Checklists

What is a Setup Sheet: A setup sheet is like a playbook for the day. It will have all of the positions in the store that need to be filled by the workers. It will have all of your registers, baggers and Drive-Thru positions labeled on it. Also, it will have everybody's shifts for the entire day. Generally the morning manager will put people in place for lunch, and the closing manager will do the same for dinner. Alternatively, it may be best for the scheduler to create the setup sheets, as they may have a certain vision of where their scheduled people should be.

Don't underestimate your setup sheet as a basic planner that just tells people where to be. You don't just throw people into spots all nilly-willy. It's a great tool for the management to not only communicate where and when everybody's supposed to be, but also play to certain people's strengths and weaknesses. I believe that a good portion of restaurants already have something like this into play, maybe on a chalk-board, dry-erase board, or it's built into the schedule itself.

If you have one, is it used effectively? I believe most managers lack the understanding of its importance – a badly written setup sheet is just begging for a bad day. A well-written setup sheet has a certain nice balance about it and will make the day feel smooth.

An Example of a Bad Setup Sheet: The training manager decides it's time for Cody to learn the Drive-Thru register. Cody has been on window for a few hours and understands the position, but just lacks practice and speed. This is his chance.

However, when Cody starts falling behind, the nearest people placed around him aren't experienced enough as well. The manager who created the setup sheet didn't think about "Who could help Cody if he fell behind?"

Probably sounds like they set themselves up for disaster, huh? Yeah, they did. If the store gets too busy and Cody can't handle it, then there's no one able to help him! The Drive-Thru starts slowing down to a crawl.

A good setup sheet would allow for the training to happen, but have a backup plan if Cody can't keep up. Guests to your restaurant should never suffer because you are trying to train. Each part of the setup sheet has to be thought through – it's not just about putting everyone in a position. You have ask yourself, "Will this setup sheet handle X amount of sales? What happens if we get even busier than that?" Picture it in your mind. Does it work out?

One Correct Way That Training Could Have Been Done: Cody works the Drive-Thru register as planned. But the setup sheet person knows that Cody is an excellent bagger as well, so why not make sure the bagger available is also a great at the Drive-Thru register as well? Then a backup plan is available, where Cody and the bagger can simply switch until your Drive-Thru speed is back to normal. The manager who created the setup sheet can even write "DT Slows Down = Switch," and draw arrows showing the two people switching positions.

How many times have you been in a similar situation where that backup plan isn't available and the store just seems to fall apart? Not everybody thinks in-depth about the day when making the setup sheet. As a matter of fact, I've been put into spots I shouldn't have been and was unable to effectively manage. I've seen other people in bad spots numerous times. Those types of days I remember being hectic for that reason.

Think Specifics: So it's important to understand the mindset to have when you're about to start writing the setup sheet. Remember to have balance. Always ask yourself questions like "What happens if this person has to step away for a few minutes? Will the surrounding workers still be able to hold it down?" At the same time, put a person in a spot they're not familiar with every now and then. You want people to grow and become more flexible – it'll certainly make your life easier down the road.

Lastly, be sure you're including actual times next to people's names when you put them in a position. Don't just write "Cody" on the Drive-Thru register slot. Instead, write "Cody 11:30-2." Not just for Cody, but for everyone in every position. When you're managing with that much attention to detail, then that's less stress for you later. Things will just flow naturally as people know what time they're supposed to be in what position. It's a nice touch that really helps the day goes smoothly.

It's relieving during shift changes to have it where the team members don't have to ask where they are for the day – they just look at the setup sheet. People clock in and people clock out nice and smoothly. It's no longer a hectic 10-15 minutes getting people into the right positions while you're supposed to be in a position yourself.

Let's move on to further achieving organization through checklists.

Getting it Done Everytime: Checklists are a great way to make sure that important tasks around the restaurant are going to be completed. Sometimes it's easy to forget a task that could impact your lunch or dinner peak. Simply forgetting to prepare a dessert could create a moment where some people have to scramble around out-of-position. A lot of these tasks can be put onto a checklist and then assigned to somebody during transition times.

Have you ever been about to start dinner and realized that somehow nobody managed to clean, dry and line the trays for guests to eat on? It's one of those "How did nobody get this done?" moments. By time you notice, it's too late and you have to frantically try to make it all work. You can almost bet on that it'll be super busy when you realize it too.

When to Prepare: What are times of the day a good amount of things around the store needs to get done? I would imagine opening, after lunch (transition phase), and closing time. You and your restaurant may have other times where things need to get done, but I can almost guarantee these three. The goal is to be preparing for busy times during slower moments – not trying to do them while it's already busy. During those busy moments you're not going to want anyone leave to grab a box of something – you want them all up front helping guests. Talk with your scheduler about insuring one person is extra to complete these checklists if possible – I suggest thirty minutes to an hour. If you're depending on this person to help guests and also get the checklist done, then they will probably fail on both ends; exception being if you work in a very low volume store.

What to Prepare: You should now have a good grasp on what time of the day a few checklists would be good for. Now you should think about what needs to be done during those times. I bet it's a good amount of things to do! Of course you have your basic stocking like cups, lids, sauces. There's also bigger stocking such as getting new boxes from the back. Brewing coffee, tea, or whatever specialty drinks you may have. You may have special stocking like refilling a salad fridge. There's probably a lot of little things that take a few minutes, and a handful of larger things that take a bigger portion of time.

Overall cleanliness such as sweeping and wiping down counters is an important one as well. Everything in your store can get messy really fast, especially after a big rush. Cleanliness cannot be ignored. I bet the dining room could use an extra hand for a few minutes to wipe down fingerprinted windows. Think about the big picture and the store as a whole. Is there anything you need to do in the kitchen on a daily basis, or maybe outside in the parking lot (i.e. a trash pickup?).

A Few Checklist Crafting Tips

1). Remember when putting these tasks on a checklist, keep it simple and clear. You want the list to be understandable by everyone – not just you. "Trays" might make sense to you, but "Dry, Line, and Place near Bagging Station" might make a bit more sense to someone who's doing the checklist for the first time. Make it dummy-proof, for a lack of a better term.

2). Having time-related goals can help push speed even when you're not there. Little details go a long way. If the checklist has 3 "parts" to it and they are allowed an hour to complete it, then you can write "9:00-9:20PM" next to the first part. Just be sure to make the time goal a realistic one – don't give them an hour's worth of tasks and tell them to get it done in 30 minutes. Put yourself in their shoes and try to imagine how long each step takes.

3). A good length is also important. I recommend trying to make the lunch transition checklist small-medium size with about 10-20 tasks to do on it. If the checklist is too long and finely detailed to the extreme, they'll be overwhelmed and most likely ignore it. Additionally, they may spend too much time actually looking at the checklist rather than getting it done. Look for parts of the checklist that could be combined. For example, instead of having two separate stocking parts for the front and drive-thru, maybe there could be just one stocking part that includes the whole store.

Other Checklist Ideas: Lastly, checklists aren't just for stocking and cleaning. They can be used for many other ideas you may have. A good idea to keep managers focused on their responsibilities is to have a personal daily or weekly checklist. The overall idea is that they complete these checklists over the week, and at the end of the week they turn it in to their GM. Of course, it doesn't need to be necessarily structured like that. Each manager could be trusted to get their work done and just use the checklist as an organizational tool.

Personal Manager Checklists: At my location, we ran with the idea of having Personal Manager Checklists on our iPad via

Gmail Documents. Each PMC had three to five tasks that needed to be done every single day. It ranged from simple manager tasks like "Did you check your e-mail today?" to "Did you take care of [X] responsibilities?" It wasn't super complex and it didn't take much time, and it did help remind managers to get things done around the store. If you have the manager turn in their checklist via paper to the GM or have it automatically sent if using an iPad/Gmail checklist, then it allows for more accountability around the store.

Overall Thoughts on Organization: Simple ideas are the best ones. I've hardly ever come up with great, big ideas and have them follow through. The reality of it is that co-workers want quick and easy ways to go about doing things. If it's something that takes too much effort, they'll skip it or try to find a shortcut around it. Think about it: If a co-manager came up to you and pitched this huge idea that would require a lot of your effort and time would you really want to get behind that? Unless it's a really great idea, you probably wouldn't. Don't you already have enough on your plate as it is? The execution part cannot be more than what the results are worth, and those types of ideas are really hard to come up with. However, if the concept of the idea is good, and the execution takes minimal effort, then it will most likely succeed.

Nothing is ever guaranteed though, and that's something you should mentally prepare yourself for. Eventually, my great idea of PMC's keeping us organized and focused eventually failed. It was mind-boggling and very frustrating. It was something I spent many hours on and a good amount of effort. I've definitely tried to run with other ideas in the past that were far-fetched and a little bit too much to handle. I couldn't help thinking, "Why did this fail?" Let's look at the concept and execution.

Concept: Personal Manager Checklists which are different for each manager. Helps them stay organized and keeps their responsibilities in check.

Execution: Simple. During your 8-hour shift you spend 5-10 minutes getting it done. Some tasks you can even delegate to another employee.

So what's wrong with this? It's a decent idea and it's not too much to think about. The only problem I can think of is that there was no sense of accountability. If somebody didn't do their PMC for a few days, what would happen? We failed on this end of it, and that's why it failed in the long run. No matter how often I reminded managers to do the PMC, it slowly failed over time. There was no serious consequence if they didn't do it. If we would have had the PMC be sent to the GM each day or week, then I don't think it would have failed. Accountability as a whole is an important fundamental to management, as we'll discuss in Chapter 4.

Getting your team to back your ideas can be tough. Sometimes people just want to work their shift and then get out. We all have those days. However, you won't last long when most of your days are like that. I accepted that my project failed not because of me, but because the people around me didn't want it to succeed. In result, my GM and I could clearly see who cared about the restaurant and who didn't. That's a good thing for the managers who finished their PMCs often and a very bad thing for those who didn't.

Closing Thoughts: In the end, organization is the ultimate key to being stress-free in the hectic world that is Quick-Service management. Our job can be very fast-paced, and you hardly want anything to ruin the workflow. Organization is the problem solver before the problem happens. So if you have too much floating around in your brain, get a notepad. If you're having trouble getting office work done in a timely manner, implement a daily folder system. If you're having trouble getting the store ready before or after a rush, craft a brand new checklist to help out.

The most important thing to remember is to never stop thinking of new ways to do old things. It's easy to dismiss organizational ideas, but in the long run it's even easier to have them in place. Try your best to think of different ways you could be doing your daily routine now. You walk in to your restaurant and you walk out, but what problems are happening between those two actions? What can you do about that? Get organized.

Chapter 3: Organization Conclusion

- **Think** about **yourself** for a minute. Are you an **organized** person at work or not? Then, how **organized** is the restaurant?
- For yourself: **Implement** organizational ideas such as notepads, daily folder systems, **and anything else** you can think of.
- For the restaurant: **Implement** setup sheets, checklists, **and anything else** you can think of.
- When bringing that organizational tool to life, think **thoroughly** about it. Think of **every little detail** from **every angle** you can.
- With your idea, **confirm** if it's **a simple or complex** idea. Will the people involved be able to get behind it? Is it an **explainable**

and **achievable** idea? Is there anything **you can do** to make it **even easier** for people to follow?

- Is there **a sense of accountability** for these new ideas? What happens if somebody just doesn't feel like doing it?

Chapter 4: Educating Others

Positional flexibility within your staff is a vital component to have. Have you ever had to run a break and the only way to make that happen was to put a completely inexperienced person in a position they've never done before? Instead of running the store, you're too tied up trying to teach or do their job for them. The newbie is trying their best, but not providing the nicest or quickest service. Meanwhile, you're stressed out because you're trying to do too many things at once – running the store, your position, and also trying to teach the newbie. It sucks, and it's not fun for anyone involved.

Unfortunately, it's also the most common and worst way people are trained. If they're lucky, maybe they get to watch a few informative training videos that at least shows them a general idea of what they're in for. But most of the time they are not scheduled as an extra person alongside an experienced trainer, and that's not good.

Think about how your training went when you were hired. What was it like? Did you get to watch training videos? Were you later tested on your knowledge? Were you buddied up with an experienced worker for the first week? How were you taught each position in the store? Did you like it or would you change the process?

Being a new person can be tough. Several people can and will quit after the first few days if they're immediately stressed out and expected to do things they weren't properly taught. It's hard enough sometimes just being surrounded by people and environment you don't know. Think about those people that quit – maybe they were secretly all-stars and would have been amazing employees down the road if given the initial proper training. Those types of people make your job easier and your restaurant better. You simply can't let those chances slip through your hands.

This chapter is not about long-term training plans, training checklists, or anything of that measure. Those ideas are good, but those are really specific to a "Training Manager" role and not applicable to everybody. Instead, I will be talking about the essence of training on-the-go. This is more of a "how to teach," rather than "here's the plan." We will go over the idea of something called perspective explaining. Afterwards, we'll explore the proper ways of correcting people. Finally we'll end it with what you can do to ensure you're doing the best job you can as a teacher.

Perspective Explaining – The Way and the Why

The way you explain a need is the most important part of that need being completed.

From the Other Side: Perspective explaining is a fancy way of saying that you're really thinking about the other person's point of view while you're teaching them – similar to empathy. You will take that new employee's perspective who has never done this specific activity before, and then very clearly explain *the way* to do it and back it up with the reason *why* they must do it.

The "way" puts them on the correct path, and the "why" keeps them on it for a long time. Let's take a moment to look over how to explain the way of doing something. Imagine you're explaining something simple like how to make an ice cream cone. Well, there are two common wrong ways a typical manager would explain that.

1. Here's the cone and a picture of the size you need to make it. Don't mess up!
   or
2. Here, watch me! – Now you do it the same way. *(Afterwards)* You need to make it bigger/smaller next time, okay?

Of course, the first example will yield the worst result. Obviously the cone will be disastrous and they won't necessarily understand whether or not if they made the right size. The second example isn't half bad, but still off. They might have watched you make a cone, but maybe they didn't learn all of the information they needed to know. It lacks an initial explaining of what's about to happen, and skips right to the demonstration.

The Way: Remember that the very words you choose are a direct impact to how well a person learns! What is my method? It is to explain every fine detail about how to make that ice cream cone. Of course, the ice cream cone may be anything: working a register, bagging food, how to count a register, etc. I figured making an ice cream cone is something simple. That, and I really like ice cream. Who doesn't?

Are you ready to make one?

"First you want to grab the cone. Make sure you only touch the paper sleeve on the cone. If you accidentally touch the cone itself, then just toss it and get a new one. You'll want to hold the cone VERY close to where the ice cream comes out. Holding it too low will make the ice cream hard to control. So when you have the cone in place, pull the lever down very slowly – it'll help from having the ice cream come out too fast. You fill the middle of the cone first, and then you'll start to see the ice cream start to smoosh.

When you see that, start going around the circle of the cone. Focus on the size while you're making the swirls. Let's say this cone is small, so we make it 2 swirls and a tip. Often times people make their cones too big with 3 swirls and a tip. Be careful! That's the wrong amount and if customers receive that size too often, they'll think that's what it's supposed to be. Also we sell thousands of ice cream cones a year, so think about how much waste that is? If you ever forget, we have pictures of the sizes right here to remind you. - Alright, it's your turn. You can make yours now and don't be afraid to mess up the first few times, it takes practice!"

Phew. That's a lot of information about a freaking ice cream cone, huh?

It sounds like over-explaining something basic, but that's the difference between bad teaching and good teaching. Every little detail is explained. It may seem like that takes a lot of time, but in reality it would only take two minutes. Those two minutes are going to determine whether or not that person makes a nice ice cream cone in 10 seconds, or takes 1 minute to make 4 bad ice cream cones and wasting product for the next few weeks or even months. Also, some newbies just hope that it'll magically get made by somebody else if they don't know how to do it properly. You got to love walking up to dessert on the screen that hasn't been made in 6 minutes yet the newbie could of easily have walked over and made it.

It will also make it easier to hold the newbie accountable in the long run if you knew you gave them the tools and information to succeed. This is very important – so give them your time and explain it right the first time. Not just with ice cream, but also with coming to work on time, properly calling out, working any other position, or absolutely anything you teach them. It's hard to catch them in the act if they didn't know any better; we'll talk more about this later.

Appreciated: A new-hire will love good teaching and patience. It will make their learning process less stressful and they won't feel out-casted. It sucks just being thrown onto a register and nobody puts time or effort into you. When you try to get outside of that bubble, you suck at everything you do because you've never been taught – or you've been taught very badly. So if you, the manager, don't feel very confident or strong in teaching, then I recommend trying to be better by really thinking about the way you explain tasks. It'll be better for you, the restaurant, and the guests.

The Why: At the end of the extraordinary ice cream cone lesson, you'll notice that I mention some things at the end that don't particularly involve the actual production of it. I explain to my trainee that the size of the cone is very important in making sure we don't mislead our guests. I also quickly mention not wasting ice cream they didn't pay for.

The reason why I mention these things is because in my job. I need to absolutely keep our numbers low in terms of costs. I can help our ice cream costs by giving the newbie some background as to why to keep making the ice cream cone correctly. This will give them a much more reason to keep making them the right size, and keep them from steering off-path.

Try to give a reason for everything you teach. Don't just give them the basics of how to make or do something, but give them a 100% explanation and tell them **WHY** to keep doing it that way. It doesn't take long, and it can be done multiple times a day. Perspective explaining is an on-the-fly mindset you can use. Now, have you ever had so much ice cream that you don't want ice cream anymore? That's how I feel about these ice cream cone explanations. So here are other examples of "the why" of things that don't have to do with ice cream.

WAY	**WHY**
Using two hands to get coins in a register instead of just one.	Can almost double your change-getting speed. Helps increase speed of service ratings.
When on the Drive-Thru headset, repeat to the guest what you are typing in as you go.	Is faster than waiting until the end and then repeating everything. Prevents from awkward "dead-air" happening. Will provide same accuracy and help all-around service.
When bagging, don't stop when you're waiting on food.	Keep bagging everything you possibly can past that in order to not have to wait on future orders. This will help speed of service to the guests. But be mindful of bagging too far ahead (no cold food!).

Making your drinks DURING the order if the drink of choice is nearby; not afterwards.	Literally trims the order-time in half and you can handle twice as many guests. Helps increase speed of service ratings.
When on the Drive-Thru window register, continue to hold a friendly conversation with the guest until the food comes up.	It's absolutely amazing service. It will also help hide the fact that you are waiting on the food.
When slow up front, instead of just only stocking/cleaning, go into the dining room to check up on guests. (Clear tables, get refills, hand out mints, chat, etc.)	Stocking and cleaning are both very important, but nothing is better than straight-up service. No guest will say "Wow, you stocked that sauce well." But they will say "Wow, this place has amazing service," and want to come back for more.

Are there other teaching ideas in your restaurant? I'm sure there are plenty. So the next time you are teaching somebody, even if it's the smallest task, try perspective explaining. Act as if you were in their shoes and think about how you would like to be taught. Explain the way how to do something very clearly and get into every little detail. Not only that, but go the extra mile by backing up that way they should do it with a good reason – they'll most likely listen and learn better. When you have a staff that you don't have to micromanage every detail because they've already been taught well, then it's a whole lot of stress off of your shoulders. You and your customers will be happier for it.

Correcting Coworkers – Unaware or Ignorant

Correcting people who do something wrong is very much the essence of your job. However, it's the most awkward and unentertaining part of your day. Bad managers avoid every little chance of confrontation. Good managers will sometimes make the corrections, but often not get their point across as well as they should. Amazing managers will promptly make the correction and in the end the person will understand completely and change their ways.

Of course, people are different. The reason why somebody doesn't understand how to do something can be different. With that said, the way you correct them needs to be different too. You can't just go bluntly correcting somebody who wasn't really aware of the correct way in the first place. Vice versa, you can't be easy-going about somebody who's playing around on their cell phone for the 3rd time that night. So where do you draw the line? How do you distinguish those differences and give the proper correction?

Unaware Co-Workers: An unaware person is somebody who doesn't know that they're doing something wrong. They have the best intent to do something correctly, but fail at it and may or may not have known the correct way in the first place. Sometimes there can be "hidden rules" that the employee may not have known about. For example, maybe not having any drips on the side of the drinks could be a big deal to you guys, but was something not brought up in training.

The ultimate key to most corrections, especially unaware do-wrongers, is the "positive than negative" approach. Where instead of just giving them a slap on the wrist for doing something wrong, you can hit them with a positive first and then the correction. What sounds better to you?

"I need you to be making your drinks during your order from here on out."
or...
"Susan, you have a great way about handling the guests. You do a really good job! I just wanted to quickly say that I think you can be making your drinks during the order. This'll make you pretty much twice as fast. Then you'll be not only super nice, but also super quick. Got it?"

You'd be surprised how rude managers can accidentally come off, even when they're generally nice people. We all know our jobs are hectic and sometimes in the heat of the battle we don't take the extra 5 seconds to pretty our words up. Again, that's the difference between a good and bad manager. You have to invest time into your coworkers – it's very important. That investment you're putting in has a very low risk and a very high reward, so why not take it?

We know how to treat co-workers who are simply unaware of their mistakes, let's move on to those who should just know better.

Ignorant Coworkers: A lot of workers in the food industry choose to do things the wrong way for numerous reasons. Often times it's a faster way of doing things, but then quality is put on the back-burner. Other times they'll blame it on a customer pressuring them. It could just be that they're a bad apple. There are many reasons why people will do things wrong, but you just have to remember one thing: Never let that be the excuse. Hear out the reason, but don't let it be the justification.

Approach them when that task has been done incorrectly. Don't be a big jerk about it, unless the problem is a big issue. It's okay to be abrupt when it's the 3rd, 4th, or 12th time somebody isn't listening. Otherwise, walk up to them politely even if they know they're doing the wrong thing. You have to be fair at least once – of course, it depends on the situation. If a coworker is blatantly rude and aggressive with a customer or even coworkers, they can find themselves promptly kicked out of the store and docked hours without a dash of politeness.

The major difference between correcting unaware coworkers and ignorant coworkers is dropping the positive out of "positive than negative." While you should be polite, don't skip over being prompt depending on the number of previous offences.

"Hey bud, I really need to chat with the guests if we have a wait on food like I told you before, okay? It really helps them forget about the wait."
and...
"Hey Sara, can you tell me how many swirls are on a large ice cream cone?" Then after they tell you the correct size, *"How many swirls did your cone have?"*

The second method is my favorite. It's socially backing them into a corner with questions until their words are contradicting their actions. It's a very neutral stance. You're feeding them basic questions and they're the ones teaching themselves. It's a good way for managers who are a little hesitant of confrontation to get their foot in the door. Don't think of it as confrontation; think of it as a conversation.

Remember that bad managers avoid confrontation. Again, it can be awkward to approach somebody and be correcting, but it is the heart of your job. For me, it's fun. Not because I like being correcting, but because I enjoy teaching and seeing results. I know several managers who struggle with this, and it gets even harder when it's a situation where you can't be so nice. However, it has to get done. The more you do it, the more it becomes natural. Otherwise, the person will just keep doing that wrong thing over and over. That's not good for anyone. That's also how the restaurant can become a little wild, in which a staff of 30 people can do a task 10 different ways. It can make your customers feel like you guys are inconsistent.

"Well another employee lets me use this coupon for another item. Why won't you?"

or...

"Why won't you let me order a catering tray within an hour? You guys let me do it last time!"

I hate getting backed into a corner by a customer because of my co-workers previous actions. I can't just blow off the guest's request and not give them what they want. So at best I can politely tell them that technically I'm not supposed to, but I'll do it for them this time. Of course, that doesn't stop them from coming in the next time and doing the same thing. Now if everyone followed the rules in the first place, then these events would happen very rarely. It's on the management to make sure everyone is on the same page about their work. That can only happen if you correct the people who need it.

One time I walked into a restaurant and ordered a meal and wanted to substitute the fries for a salad. I wound up getting charged for both and receiving both, even though I only wanted the salad. I went back to the front counter, explained my situation and was promptly told that "it saved me money" by a relatively newer employee. I fought a little harder and was told the same thing again. Long story short, I didn't get a refund for the fries I didn't want. I got fed up and just suffered the money loss. I wonder how many customers she did the same thing to afterwards until a manager finally confronted her about it.

Before this chapter ends, I wanted to go over some brief teaching tips that may help you get a grasp on working with your coworkers.

Teaching Tidbits

Don't be a negative teacher: Managers are hardly taught how to correct and teach people. Instead they're taught how to count drawers, open or close the store, etc. Teaching for whatever reason gets forgotten about, even though it's so vital to your job. Because of this, teaching usually comes off in a negative and inexperienced way. If they have the guts to correct people at all, they usually attack the person about what they did wrong. That works sometimes, but it also doesn't make either person feel good about the situation. Be a positive teacher. Teaching can be a fun and influential part of your job when you do it right. You can use the ideas and thoughts we discussed earlier in the chapter to help push positive teaching. You should only be negative if the situation is drastic enough to call for it.

If you're more focused on their long-term personal growth because you care, then that person will notice and respect you for it. Don't just be about putting people down. That creates a hard leader to follow.

Take deep breaths and have lots of patience: Some people just don't learn quickly, or just don't get it. In our industry, we get a lot of young people who've never had jobs before. Consequently, I often have to re-explain my expectations to over and over. I might have to teach them to make that dreaded ice cream cone five times over for a week until they finally make one correctly. Teaching can take a chunk of time, and it's really easy to give up on a person. But remember, the small time investment of stepping in and teaching now saves time later.

Some people react to different tones of a teaching: Think about each "tone" you might use in the next couple of situations. If Henry has had several jobs before, seems to be grasping things quickly and has an eagerness to learn, I might be more laid-back during teaching. He's clearly getting it, so let's make the job fun. But if Tamika has never worked in this environment before and is struggling to learn simple tasks, I might want to stay professional and use "positive/negative" teaching to help reinforce motivation. Of course, if Devon is coming in late once or twice a week and always complains about what position we put her in, I should probably be very clear with her with my expectations and make sure she understands that I'm serious.

In the end, teaching styles always need to be adjusted because everyone learns differently. So treat each coworker individually and understand that you may need to change your methods to get the best results. If you stay the same, not everyone will be able to learn from you. But if you adjust your ways, they might be able to benefit more from it and it could help them to learn faster.

Enjoy Teaching: I used to hate it, but now I love teaching. The more my role forced me to do it, the more I appreciated the effort that goes into it. The difference you make in that person is the true payoff. Now anytime I see somebody doing something wrong, I know how to approach to the situation – you should too.

The more time and work you put into teaching, the easier your job becomes. If you're looking for more respect from your coworkers around the store, this is the key to that. This is the biggest stepping stone from "just another manager" to a leader and a boss. Teaching not only helps the co-worker, but it also helps you too. It's nice to be able to just work a position and not have to help a coworker every 5 minutes. Because of so, the store can flow smoother and the staff becomes faster and better. In the end, isn't that what your job is all about?

Chapter 4: Educating Others Conclusion

- **Practice "Perspective Explaining,"** in which you explain **every little detail** about the task and **make your expectations known.**
- Remember **to back up your "ways"** with the **"why"** to do it that way. This will ensure **long-term success** for that task getting done.
- Correcting an employee who's simply **unaware** of their mistake? Apply the **"positive and then negative" technique.**
- Correct an employee who's **ignorant** and not listening? Drop the positive and **be prompt** about your expectations.
- **Don't be a negative teacher** by attacking your coworkers with a correction. **Teach them kindly** unless the situation calls for you to step up and be strict.
- **Have patience** and expect to reteach easy tasks and re-explain your expectations. **Reiteration is sometimes frustrating,** but it's also good for teaching.

- **Be aware** of your **tone and attitude** when teaching. **Be relaxed** with go-getters and **be strict** with potential "bad eggs." **Never joke around** with people who are intentionally being disrespectful.

Chapter 5: Reinvent Yourself & Never Settle

If there's one thing to take away from this book, it's that time usually raises expectations. The more time that has passed, the more demand in productivity and skills as a leader. Consequently, it's easy to get worn out and unfocused as time passes by. Maybe at the beginning you felt focused and invigorated to get your job done. You felt like a real go-getter and had all of this energy and passion to get things done. That's great!

The sad reality is that it doesn't last forever. After all, we are all human. Understand that it's okay to feel this way. You will have a day where you wake up and would rather do anything but go to work. You will have a week where you just want to clock out the *minute* you're schedule off and not stay extra during busy moments or to get office work done.

It's called burnout. It's where you've busted your butt for months on end and you could just use a break. We all experience it, but the tricky part is that we all different ways of solving it.

What generally helps me is to get away from work for small periods of time and often. I frequently take little two-day vacations every month with my wife. It took me a while to figure out what worked best for me. Before, I tried taking a week off about twice a year, but found the long stretch of working to be too much. I'd start feeling burnt out, and then still have two or three months left. After all this is a high-paced job where you're on your feet all day long and moving fast as possible for long periods of time.

Working through a true burnout can be pretty horrible for both the employee and the business. Talk about all-time low productivity and all of your passion drained.

The purpose of getting away is to get out of the traditional day-in and day-out work flow, and to just take a relaxing weekend trip. Sounds nice already, right? When you come back, you'll have a lot more energy built up and feel more refreshed. I don't know about you, but by time I'm back from the weekend vacation I feel a little unproductive. It makes me a little more excited to get back to work – back out into the real world.

So what's your reset button?

The theme of our final chapter is to discover yourself at a low-point in your job and to get re-focused, re-energized, and re-motivated. I call this reinventing yourself. It's not only something you should do when you are at a low-point, but something you should do often in order to keep yourself progressing as a better leader. Afterwards, we will talk about how settling for less-than-competent employees can be a true killer of greatness. What makes an employee incompetent? How do you deal with them? When do you pull the plug and look for a more talented employee? We'll cover all of that ahead.

Reinventing Yourself

It's Important: This is the crucial never-ending fundamental that helps you continuously revaluate yourself and make sure you're not falling behind. If Chapter's 1-4 are the cake, then this is the icing that keeps you going for years to come.

Figure Out Where Are You Now: A tricky part of leadership is evaluating your own performance and trying to see where you can grow. That's because there are so many components to leadership and management that it's hard to find a place to start.

A good start point is to look at your other co-managers and ask yourself, "What are they better at than me?" Might sound a little harsh, but be objective about it – this might help you understand and find a weaknesses of your own. I advise you write these down in that notepad you've bought. It's nice to check your notepad and remember, "Oh yeah, I need to make sure I'm working on training people when it's slow more often," or whatever idea you think of. Alternatively, you can meet with your bosses and they can help you, as mentioned before in Chapter 2: Self Goals.

In case you need more ideas of where you might be able to grow, here are two examples of commonly found managers that could reinvent themselves in one way or another.

Catch-Up Charlie: Charlie was promoted several months ago and is one of the newest members of the management staff. He's well past his initial management training and takes care of money responsibilities without a problem. However, when it's time to shine as a leader, he doesn't pep-talk the crew, train people when it's slow, or drive the focus of the restaurant. He may feel a little out of place at times, but his co-managers are just begging for some initiative from him. Charlie needs to reinvent himself, which would make him realize he's learned the role of a manager, but he has low leadership skills and is barely doing the basics. It's time to play catch-up.

Sleepy Sam: Sam has a few years of management under his belt. Back in the day, he was considered one of the best leaders in the restaurant and ran the store with an energizing passion. Nowadays, he's average and isn't excited as he used to be about his role. He may still push and try to motivate others, but only if the situation calls for it and not out of free will. He ignores his work e-mail and always seems out of the loop. He's severely burnt out and it's time for a reinvention. Sam should take a small vacation with the idea to come back and reinvent himself on the first day of his return.

He has the skills to be a leader, but he needs to find his lost passion. Sam should take just 30 minutes to an hour and think about what areas he wants to improve. Once he does that, he should be refreshed, refocused, and excited to be a leader. It's time to wake up.

How do we do that and what does that exactly mean? Keep on reading, we'll get there. First, let's look at the glaring problems with both of these managers. They may be fictional, but maybe these characters are more real than you know.

How to Reinvent: Reinventing yourself is not an easy task to achieve. It's a very mental-intensive hurdle you have to force yourself to jump over. It's very similar to breaking bad habits. Imagine if you didn't want to lock your car doors after you got in your vehicle. In order to change, you really have to THINK and TRY to not lock your car doors every single time. It will feel against your nature for a while and unfamiliar. It takes time, patience, self-awareness, and most of all the willpower to do so.

1.) **Ask Yourself Truthfully:** What does getting better at your job mean to you? Would you feel more confident and calm in situations? Would you possibly benefit from potentially making more money? Are you excited to learn more and teach others around you? Will the job skills you learn here help you if you got your dream job? Maybe this job means you can support your spouse, pay off a car or to be able to have spending money. Find questions that you can say "yes" to, which could spark at least a little motivation. This should be a moment where you take the necessary time to remember why you're here in the first place. Take a healthy 10 minutes to think of these reasons – I recommend writing these down for yourself.

2.) **Relooking At Your Goals:** If you don't have any short to mid-term goals –something achievable within the next 3 months— then you need to get some. We covered this immensely in Chapter 2: Self Goals, so please revisit it you need help. Again, goals are crucial to giving you something to aim for each and every day you go to work. If you already have goals, then you need to find new ones that will motivate you more. Brainstorm for a little bit and think of a new tasks or responsibility that excites you. Make it a concrete, achievable goal.

3.) **The Grass is Always Greener:** We always want what we don't have. It can be hard to appreciate your time at work. Try to take time to enjoy the positives. Do you really love some of your co-workers? Perhaps you were given an award of recognition in the past. Maybe your job is comfortable with availability changes and requesting days off. Take a moment and really soak that stuff in. It's the little things that can make you appreciate what you have. It's easy for the joys of your current workplace to lose their flare over time. Try to keep your feet on the ground and love where you're at – don't always have your head in the clouds.

4.) **Sit Down and Just Talk:** You need to tell your bosses. It might sound like you're digging your own grave, but in my case it actually gives the opposite effect. Sit down with someone and let them know, "I'm having a hard time getting motivated to do well here." Plan to sit down for thirty minutes or so. In those thirty minutes, a lot of good will come out. They can give you reasons, ideas and angles about your role that you maybe didn't think about before. Maybe you'll come to find you're much more appreciated than you thought, and that alone will push you to a new high.

5.) **Take action & Speak Up:** It's the most important part. Put a lot of brainpower into trying to constantly stay self-aware of how you are doing. For example, is the dinner rush starting to roll in? You know that you generally stay quiet. Instead, try to actually pump up the staff to make them aware of how busy it actually is. It doesn't take much, just a little "Alright guys, it's game time," can change the focus of the team as well as making your presence known. Make sure the kitchen staff has everyone in position and is ready to go. Quickly pump up each person in each position. Remember to have this mentality with **everything** you do.

6.) **Reflect:** Take time to look back and ask yourself, "Did I make the right moves?" or "What could have I done differently?" If you spend a minute and can't think of any better ways, chances are you made the right calls. Be proud of that! Do this every day and even during your shift if you have time to. If you say to yourself "Maybe I should have spoken up..." or "I should have ran that break earlier before the dinner rush hit," or anything along those lines, that's not a bad thing! Realizing your potential is a half-step to getting to where you want to be. Convince yourself that you'll certainly make the effort the next time the opportunity arises.

Does reinventing yourself sound scary? It can be – change is scary to most people. Do you know what's scarier? Being stuck at a job and never pushing yourself to grow from it, and not being good enough to make decent money. Then leaving after several years and looking back and feeling like it was a waste of time.

Reinventing yourself should be done every few months and can prevent this from happening. At least twice a year.

You could feel like you need to push yourself as a leader more often like Catch-Up Charlie. You could feel like you need to get re-motivated like Sleepy Sam. You could feel like you are your own character with your own problems. No matter where you fit, you're taking on a big challenge during what might be a hard time. But when are things usually reinvented upon? When they are out of date or just don't serve their original purpose anymore.

What is The Point of Reinventing Myself?: The goal of reinventing yourself is to catch yourself during a low moment and throwing yourself back on top of performance. Even if you're not at a low-point, it's a good check-in with yourself to make sure you are still doing a good job. It will also test you to meet challenging goals and learn as much as you can from your job. Consider it like getting over a speed bump, a hill, or a mountain of issues. Most importantly, reinventing yourself in the eyes of your bosses looks like your improving, whereas waiting until your boss approaches you about not meeting their standards looks like you're doing badly. Beat them to it.

Why is This a Fundamental of Management? – I don't blame those who seem skeptical on why this is a fundamental. Simply put, it's easy to get lazy and comfortable at work. The reason why I stress this subject so strongly is because I truly believe that laziness is the true killer of most people in their jobs. Reinventing yourself in a timely manner will prevent this from happening. You perform at work every day and everyone around you sees that. Taking a big step back and looking at yourself in a critical manner is crucial to recognizing where you can improve. Without this fundamental, everything you learn becomes wasted because you will become too unmotivated to use it.

This may be shocking, but many employees in the world have it backwards. They might have an idea of reinventing themselves if their boss pays them more. It's the typical "pay me and then I'll work harder" mentality. That doesn't sound too crazy – you *should* earn more money for the harder you work. We've been trained to think this way most of our lives. The reality of that is the opposite. Think of it as a "work harder then I'll pay you more" policy. Since your boss is the one making the decisions on your pay rate, maybe you should listen to their policy, and not yours.

Also, we as humans naturally prefer to stay comfortable and avoid change. It's easy to learn management basics and never progress from there. The lure of being comfortable is very tempting, but then self-progression will slow down to a crawl or become non-existent. Progression is something that you have to be active and self-aware about. You won't progress by just clocking in, doing the basics, and clocking out. Between clocking in and out, there has to be a tremendous, real conscious and self-aware effort to change and progress. Stay fresh; don't become stale.

Never Settle

What is Settling: The poison that slowly kills most restaurants. Where reinventing is all about yourself, settling is all about the people around you. Settling is that moment where you see a co-worker with no passion or just doesn't "get it" and nothing is done to help the issue. "It" could be giving guests poor service; not showing up on time; not able to keep up with the speed of the job; disrespecting co-workers or guests, etc. "It" could be anything. Settling is the feeling of seeing an issue that's directly affecting the restaurant's quality and turning your head the other way.

Have you ever had a talk or two with an employee about something they did wrong, yet they still continue to do it? Then nothing gets done about it? Or not even having that talk in the first place? That's settling.

Have you ever had something in the store that almost always goes wrong such as catering orders? Then nothing gets done about it? That's settling.

When you settle for less, you receive less.

Unfortunately, settling is a very easy thing to. But why is it easy? I'm sure most of these co-workers aren't bad people. The majority of people you work with are generally nice people – they have had to do well in the interview in the first place, right? The issue lies with management not wanting to look past that. While I've never been a true believer in the expression "You're only as good as your weakest link," having too many weak links in the chain who aren't capable of certain job requirements can definitely hold back the team's potential.

Recognizing and Treating Incompetent Employees: Bernice is a very nice woman who takes care of each and every guest extraordinary well. She always shows on time and rarely calls out. However, there's one aspect of the job she is extremely poor at: speed. She is miserably slow. She's the last person to count on when there's a rush of guests suddenly standing in line. Everybody knows she's the slowest, but nobody does anything about it. But she does a great job with the guests, so what's the big issue?

Imagine a guest's point of view. You walk in the door and wait way too long in line. By time you get to the counter to place your order, maybe service isn't what you want so much anymore. Next time you'll go to the restaurant across the street.

Now what if you could have both exceptional service AND speed? Well, believe it or not... you can! Imagine if you're entire team was filled with all-stars who were fast, independent, dependable, and pleasant. Wouldn't that be amazing?

It's not impossible. Matter of fact, there are several ways to achieve that goal.

1). **Invest Time & Training:** Perhaps the key ingredient that is missing is just training. Bernice gives amazing service because of her extremely nice personality. However, has the team truly invested any time in teaching her speed? It may take a few days, a couple hours each, to really make her understand the way and the why of really cranking out a line. In the long run, won't that investment be worth it? This is the most common solution to these types of issues.

2). **Play Strengths/Reposition:** Maybe during training it's clear that it just wasn't meant to be: Bernice will always be slow. Something in her just won't "click." Are there any positions where we could utilize those strengths and also hide weaknesses? For this instance, perhaps being a dining room hostess would be a perfect fit. If it solves the problem and makes the restaurant better for it, then it's the right move.

3). **Replacement:** Usually this is where people decide to settle. Most businesses will stop here and not take measures needed to fix the problem. If you have invested time and effort into Bernice, repositioned her or can't find a new position for, then it's time to part ways. This is a crucial step, but it can be necessary. Maybe this job just isn't for Bernice. Is it fair to either side if she stays? Ask yourself: what is the end-goal and vision of the restaurant in the next few months? Do you see that employee in that picture? If the answer is no, then it's time to move on and find somebody who can be.

I immediately apologize to all of the Bernice's in the world. Obviously, Bernice can be anybody you work with. "Bernice" may really have different strengths and weaknesses. That's the point. Maybe at your restaurant you have one, two, or even five "Bernice's." It's time to act.

Speak Up – Be a Boss: The most common form of settling is being uninvolved in fixing problems. Whether the issue is simple or complicated, you can't just turn your head and ignore it. Otherwise, who else is going to fix that problem? Maybe it's a good chance for you to act as a leader. Over my years I've often seen co-workers who clock in late without a single manager even confronting the situation. Perhaps they come back from break 5 minutes late every day. Now it's a big deal because nobody has stepped up to talk with them. They've settled and decided it is okay for that to happen.

Complicated issues may include more serious offenses: several callouts, language/attitude around the workplace, disrespecting guests or employees, etc. The issue may not even be a person; it could be something related to your day-to-day operations at the restaurant. Maybe you think there's a better way to do something – you'll never know until you speak up.

Help with the solution of the problem – don't just whine and complain to others. Whatever it takes to fix the problem, then that's the route to take. Speak up. Being a problem solver is an amazing way to get noticed by your bosses. But remember to do it as a team if possible – don't shove other people out of the way just so you can shine. You're in this for the long-run after all, so don't shoot yourself in the foot for your future's sake.

The customers, employees, and the value of the restaurant suffer each time you don't speak up. Settling is saying that there is a problem right here in front of me and I'm not going to do anything about it – even though you are one of the few who actually can.

About People: If it is a minor issue is caused by a co-worker, then you need to speak to them. Always treat them with kindness and respect. Remember how we phrase our corrections with a "positive and then negative" approach. If it is a major issue caused by a co-worker, then the situation may cause for a more direct approach. You should never yell or scream at an employee – that can get you in trouble. Stay civil and talk it out calmly.

About the Restaurant: If the issue is systematic or a general "way about things" that just isn't working or could be improved, then talk to other management about your new idea. If you can get support on a new idea, then it's safe to go to your boss and try to change it. Even if you didn't get support, others around you and your bosses will appreciate that you're thinking in that direction. It's important to see how your co-managers think though, because you wouldn't want the idea to backfire and only you to be blamed.

Outro: Simply showing effort and interest is a key ingredient in impressing your bosses. Anyone can be taught how to count drawers or open and close the store. It's the hungry mindset that strives to be better. The people who push for being better truly worth keeping around. The one who doesn't settle is the same who will always be progressing. So don't get stuck, because you won't go forward.

Chapter 5: Reinventing Yourself and Never Settle
Conclusion

- **Understand** that **time changes expectations** and it is **your goal** to always keep up.
- **Before** taking on the big task of reinventing yourself, **take a few days off** and clear your mind. Come back feeling **energized** and **re-motivated.**

- **Evaluate yourself** and find **your leadership weaknesses.** How and where can you **grow** the most?
- **Take** the **Six Steps** of Reinvention: **Ask yourself** what this job **means**; **relook** at short to mid-term **goals**; **appreciate** where you are **now**; **talk** with your **bosses**; **take more action** and **speak up**; reflect on **your day's work.**
- **Understand** what **settling** is and **recognize** that you are the **one of few** who can make **changes** in your restaurant.
- Spend time **training** employees to be **better** or **reposition** them in order to **play** to their **strengths** and avoid unfixable **weaknesses.** If all else **fails,** consider finding a **replacement.**
- **Never** turn your head the other way. **Approach issues** and always be as **polite** as the situation calls for.

After Thoughts

Work is Hard: What you can do for yourself in the meantime is set goals, learn, and try your hardest. If you're at work for 40 hours a week, why not make those hours really count? Don't just do the bare minimum; go the extra mile. That's what I've learned in my life and it's taken me farther than most. Not just as a manager at a restaurant, but as a husband to my wife; a son to my mother and father; a human to society, and so on and so forth.

I've seen a lot of people come and go at my workplace. I've worked with about 200+ different employees over my years. I've spent a lot of time learning every little thing that I can and doing my best job to improve every single day. I still am. I'm glad that I have spent a lot of time passing on my knowledge and doing my best to grow the people around me. Those people have grown and became managers. Some of them have grown and found the one job they really wanted. I'm happy to play a part in that and help pave the way.

I've helped countless guests in my restaurant. I hope that I treated each and every one the way I would like to be treated. When I'm not there, I'm confident my crew is doing their best and giving equal service. It's such a joy walking into a restaurant – in a good mood or not – and getting exceptional service and speed. I'm glad to know that I've been a part of the bigger picture in making that happen. It can seriously turn a person's day around.

Most of all I'm glad that I have others that hold me accountable. These are my bosses and co-management team who push me to be the best I can. They are my motivators. Without motivation in life, it's extremely easy to get lazy. Thanks to that, I've been allowed to see the rewards that life can give you when you contribute the time and effort.

I hope that you will too. I hope that this book has given you at least these two things:

1.) A new desire to create goals for yourself. To meet new challenges and design a plan to conquer them.
2.) To feel motivated to complete these goals. To have the willpower and energy to execute said plans.

If you look back at where you were two years ago, do you feel embarrassed at all? Perhaps it could be compared to looking at old photographs of yourself wearing out-of-date clothing or funny glasses. Of course, in the moment you had every right to feel okay about yourself. But I think if you don't feel embarrassed in retrospect, then you haven't changed much. I *want* to feel a little silly thinking about myself back then, because that means I feel so much knowledgeable in my life now.

Thank you for reading.

"Be the change that you wish to see in the world."
- Gandhi

If you've made it this far, please do me a favor and leave a review on my Amazon page! This will help other potential leaders find my book and could help them grow. I would also love to know what you thought of the book.

http://www.amazon.com/Leadership-5-Fundamentals-Restaurant-Managers/dp/1500723886/ref=sr_1_1?ie=UTF8&qid=1443413656&sr=8-1&keywords=Brent+Boso

I greatly appreciate you taking the time out of your life to read my book. It comes from the heart and I did my best to respect your time and keep it direct. Many books ramble on forever and favor quantity of pages over quality. Having a journalistic background, my goal is always to get the most amount of information in the least words of possible. I hope you enjoyed.

Thanks for reading!

Brent Boso

Made in the USA
Middletown, DE
02 December 2017